colorful
creatures

stickers and activities

colorful
creatures
stickers and activities

Anita Ganeri and Penny Arlon

weldon**owen**

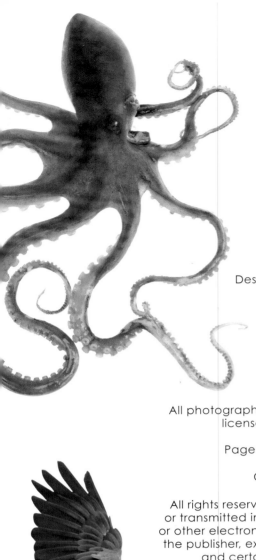

weldon**owen**

Authors: Anita Ganeri and Penny Arlon

Design: Tory Gordon-Harris, Natalie Schmidt, Anna Pond

Editorial: Lydia Halliday, Susie Rae

Fact checker: Tom Jackson

Art Director: Stuart Smith

Publisher: Sue Grabham

Insight Editions Publisher: Raoul Goff

All photographs in this book including those used on the cover are used under license from Shutterstock.com with the following exceptions:
Page 10, "Crab" © chiravan39/iStock
Page 36, "Pygmy Blue Whale" © Franco Banfi/naturepl.com

Published by Weldon Owen Children's Books

An imprint of Weldon Owen International, L.P.

A subsidiary of Insight International, L.P.

PO Box 3088
San Rafael, CA 94912

www.insighteditions.com

ISBN: 978-1-68188-740-1

Printed in China

First printed in 2020

24 23 22 21 20 1 2 3 4 5

Contents

Look for the fun activities in each chapter. There are mazes, dot to dots, word searches, sticker scenes, and more!

Find the giant poster and sticker sheets at the end of the book!

Hello Color

Red, yellow, brown, pink, purple, blue, and orange—animals come in all sorts of colors. Some animals are brightly colored while other animals are harder to spot. Their colors are not simply for showing off. In nature, colors and patterns help animals to stay alive.

Some colors help animals to blend into the background for protection. While certain colors help animals to send signals to each other. This allows the animals to keep in touch and even find a mate. Bright colors are often warning signs that an animal tastes horrible or is poisonous.

Many animals have more than one color or pattern. They may be multicolored or have mixtures of stripes, splotches, and spots. These markings look strong and striking, but they also confuse attackers who find the animals difficult to see and catch. A few animals can even change color so that they can hide in different places, and also show their feelings.

In this book, you will meet animals of many colors, from striking black-and-white zebras to stunning emerald-green lizards. See if you can guess what they use their colors for.

Red

Many insects use mimicry to hide from predators or attract prey. This means they pretend to be something that they are not—like a disguise! The red leaf beetle, for example, is not poisonous, but a bird might avoid eating it because it looks similar to the poisonous ladybug.

Ladybugs

Grouper fish

Butterfly

Dart frog

Butterfly

Golden net-wing beetles

Scarlet lily beetle

Indonesian beetles

Butterfly

Milk snake

Butterfly

Red velvet mites

Bamboo snake

Firebug

Calico snake

Cardinal

Crab

Moontail bullseye fish

Seed tick

Bigeye fish

Red palm weevils

Betta fish

Bigeye fish

Australian
king parrot

Indonesian
beetle

Potato
beetle

Sea star

Scarlet ibis

Scarlet
lily
beetle

Ladybug

Parrotfish

Stonefish

Betta fish

Cardinal
lory

Sea star

Scarlet ibis

Cichlid fish

Butterfly

Red velvet mites

Seed ticks

Ladybird spider

Sea star

Bullfinch

Rooster

Red squirrel

Velvet ant

Betta fish

Strawberry finch

Bullfinch

Ark clams

Bearded dragons

Scallops

Monkfish

Great frigatebird

Colorado beetles

Velvet ants

Betta fish

Turkey

Milk snake

Sharp-nosed
crab

Stag beetle

Hermit crab

Lady beetles

Cardinal

Tomato frog

Yellow-bibbed lory

Macaw

Panther chameleon

Firebugs

Butterfly

Mandrill

Coral snake

Poplar leaf beetle

Red snappers

Sockeye salmon

Flashy red

Get ready for these bright red puzzles. But be warned, some animals are red to show they taste bad or are even poisonous!

Spot the difference

Can you find two differences between these wiggly milk snakes?

WATCH OUT!

The ladybug has a cunning trick. It oozes a nasty-tasting goo from its knees! The red color warns other animals that it tastes bad.

What comes next?

Look at the animal patterns. Can you work out which red animal comes next on each line?

Use your stickers here!

Draw the other half

Copy the patterns to complete the butterflies.

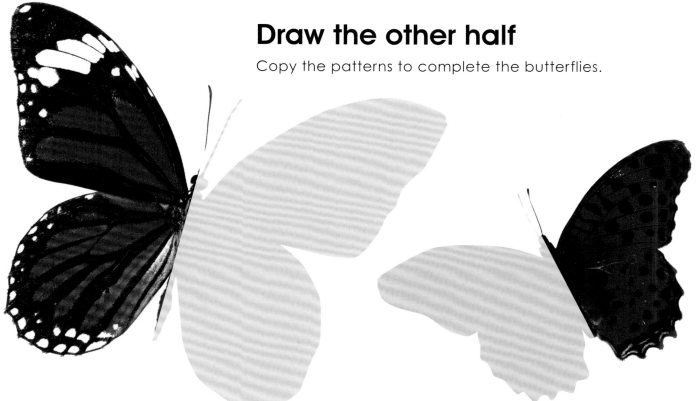

Color me in

Use different shades of red to color in the striped fish.

Which has the most spots?

One of these ladybugs has more spots than the others. Can you spot it?

LOOK AT ME!

The male frigate bird puffs out its bright red chest to attract a mate.

16

Who likes shrimp?

Follow the lines to find out which bird eats shrimp.

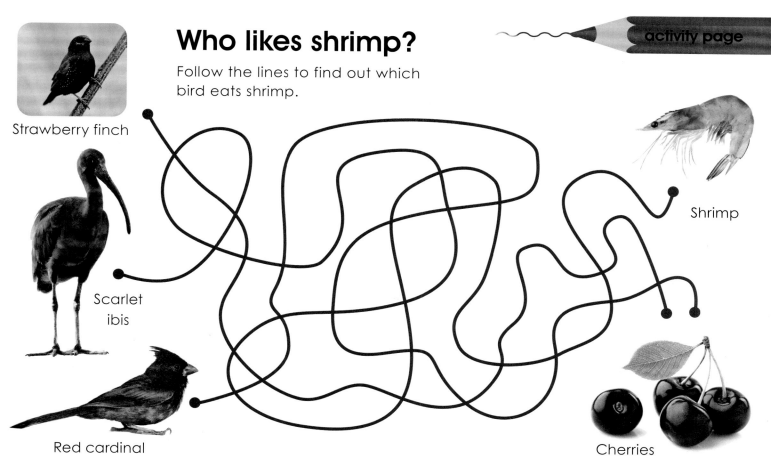

Strawberry finch

Scarlet ibis

Red cardinal

Shrimp

Cherries

Sticker scene

How many red crabs can you find on your sticker sheet?
Fill the beach with red crabs!

Use your stickers here!

Orange

Orange animals, such as Monarch butterflies, are easy to spot. But their bright color sends a message to hungry birds. It tells them to stay away—these butterflies are horrible to eat.

Cat

Sea stars

Corn snake

Sea slug

Sea urchin

Gila monster

Grasshoppers

Orangutan

Newts

Tomato frog

Slug

Crab

Clownfish

Caterpillar

Monarch butterflies

Llama

Stag beetle

Atlas moth

Cock-of-the-rock

Butterflies

Tiger

Pigeon
blood
discus fish

Kitten

Bearded dragon

Tarantula

Scorpion

Hummingbird

Goldfish

Parakeets

21

Scarlet minivet

Macaws

Silk moth

Owl

Butterfly

Giant firefly

Box turtle

Piglets

Ants

Bat

Discus fish

Telescope goldfish

Hamster

Octopus

Sika deer

Toucan

Tiger

Discus fish

Cat

Monarch butterflies

Rabbit

Tree frogs

Tomato frog

Red crab

French bulldog

Blue-winged pitta

Killifish

Dhole

Sika deer

Tree frog

Pufferfish

Tarantula

Clownfish

Fiery orange

Close your eyes and think of three different orange animals. They could be furry or scaly, big, or small. Are they on this page?

Mini-beast mix up!

Can you find four ants, three butterflies, two caterpillars, and one cricket?

FLOWER POWER

The African queen butterfly is a tasty snack for a bird. The orange butterfly sits on an orange flower to hide, or camouflage.

Word search

These orange animals are all in the word grid. Can you find them?

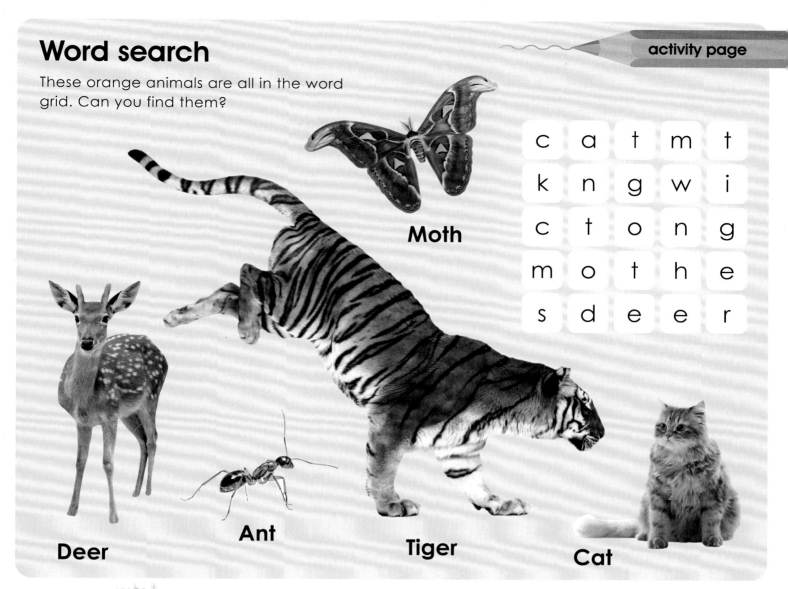

c	a	t	m	t
k	n	g	w	i
c	t	o	n	g
m	o	t	h	e
s	d	e	e	r

Moth

Deer

Ant

Tiger

Cat

Maze

The orange kitten is searching for its favorite toy. Can you help it find its way?

start

finish

Matching pairs

Look carefully. Can you find two newts that are exactly the same?

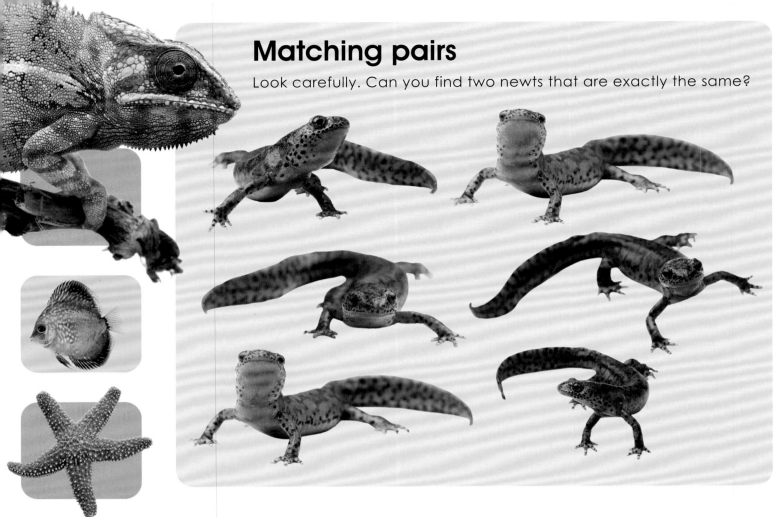

Odd one out

Look at the shoal of orange clown fish. Which one doesn't match the others?

HIDDEN TIGER

A tiger's orange stripes help it to hide in the grass. The tiger hides so it can creep up on the animal it hunts.

Follow the lines

The orangutans are very hungry. Which one will reach its favorite fruit?

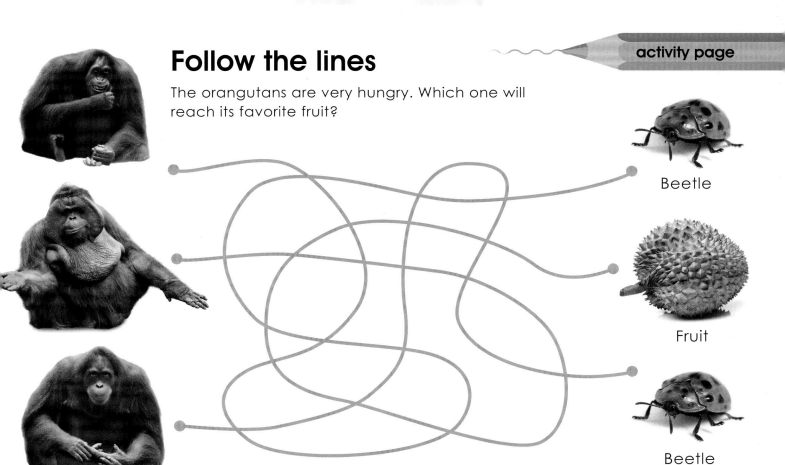

Beetle

Fruit

Beetle

How many left?

Each flower can only have one butterfly land on it. How many butterflies will need to keep fluttering?

Yellow

When wild animals are bright yellow, they attract a lot of attention. Birds use this flashy shade to impress their mates, while insects and reptiles warn off predators. Darker yellows and golds are great for blending into deserts and dry grass, hiding local animals like lions from their prey.

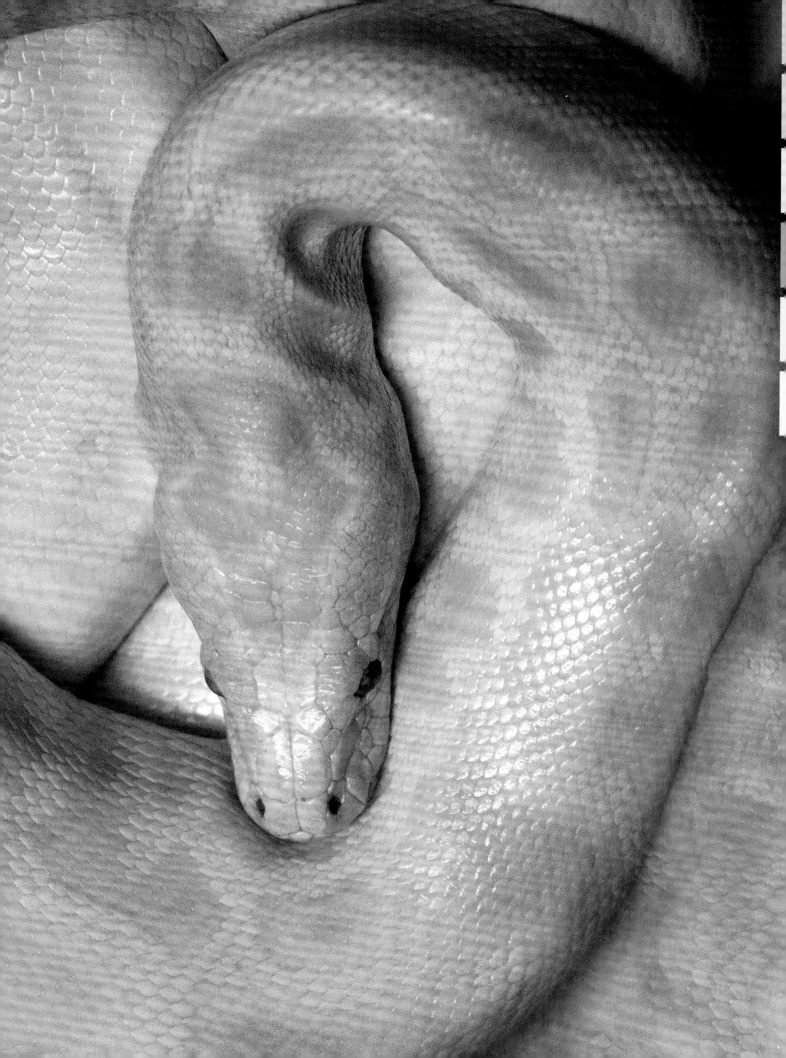

Parakeets

Seahorses

Chicks

Fire salamander

Viper

Yellow weevils

Crab spider

Tree frogs

Banana slug

Bearded dragon

Python

Brain sponge

Yellow tang

Trevally fish

Butterflyfish

Land crab

Coal tit

Weaver bird

Wasps

Orange tip
butterflies

Box fish

Cane
toads

Lion cub

Snails

Golden
poison frog

Gold ram fish

Leopard gecko

Canary

Monarch butterflies

Sunbird

Butterfly

Corn snakes

Trumpet snails

Yellow tang

Ladybugs

Cheetah

Butterflies

Ducklings

Macaw

Emperor penguins

Parakeet

Crabs

Sun parakeet

Butterflies

Sea anemone

Tree frog

Grove snails

Python

Lion

Foxface rabbitfish

Axolotl

Labrador retriever puppy

Butterflies

Sunny yellow

How many yellow animals can you see on these pages? You'll need to unscramble, spot, and search to solve the puzzles.

Help the buzzing bee

The bee wants to buzz to the biggest yellow flower. Which path should it choose?

DEADLY YELLOW

The golden poison dart frog is one of the most poisonous animals in the world. Its yellow color warns "don't eat me!"

Find the shadows

The yellow animals have lost their shadows!
Can you find them?

Dot to dot

Connect the dots,
starting at number 1.
Which super-slow,
yellow animal
will appear?

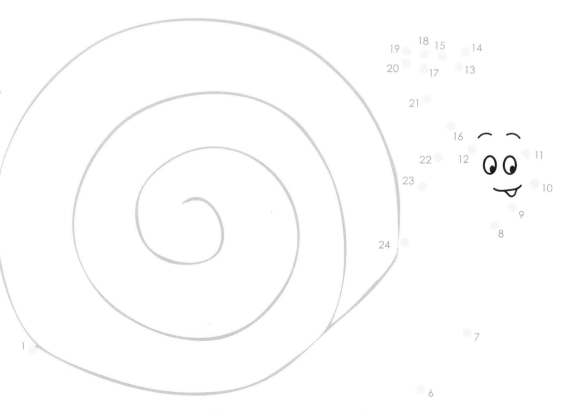

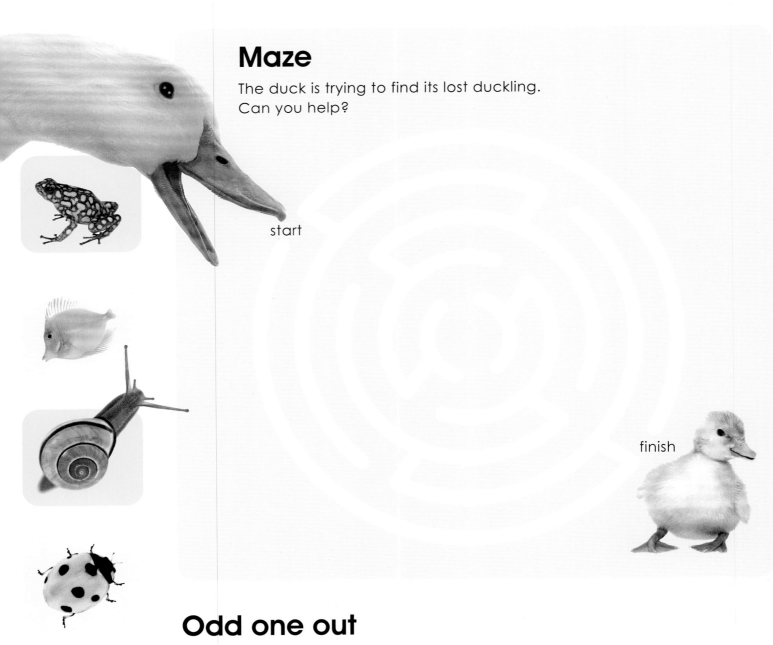

Maze

The duck is trying to find its lost duckling.
Can you help?

start

finish

Odd one out

Look carefully at the golden beetles. Which one doesn't match the others?

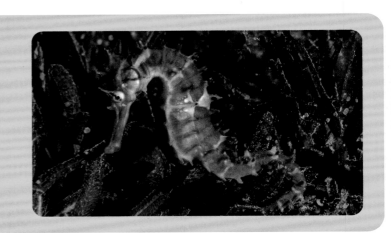

COLOR CHANGE

This yellow seahorse has a neat trick. It can make its skin darker to hide among sea plants.

Draw the other half

Draw and color in the other half of the crab.

Word search

Can you find the yellow animals in the word grid?

t	c	u	b	s
f	i	s	h	n
r	d	l	l	a
o	m	u	n	i
g	t	g	f	l

Fish

Slug

Frog

Snail

Cub

37

Green

For hiding among leaves and undergrowth, green is the perfect disguise. It allows this little lizard to sneak up on juicy insects to eat. The insects don't see the lizard until it is too late.

Leaf mimic katydid

Scarab beetle

Damselfish

Red-eyed tree frog

Gecko

Butterfly

Grasshopper

Swallowtail caterpillar

Eastern green mamba

Shining pot beetles

Egyptian green toad

Parrotfish

Crocodile

Tree frog

Butterfly

Butterfly

Flower beetle

Terrapin

Bearded dragon

Caterpillar

Mantis

Arboreal lizard

Lanternfly

Praying mantis

Green parrot

Parakeet

Chameleon

Parrotfish

Luna moth

Dead-nettle leaf beetle

Flower beetle

Butterfly

Grasshopper

Dead-nettle leaf beetle

Figeater beetles

Machaon caterpillar

Caterpillar

Woodboring beetle

Long-horned grasshoppper

Leafhopper

Beetle

Leaf insect

Fire-bellied toad

Leaf insect

Beetle

Spinefoot fish

Hawksbill turtle

Green lizard

Flower beetle

Butterfly

Lizard

Tortoise

Chameleon

Cichlid

Green shield bugs

Hummingbird

Pike

Fire-tufted barbet

Frog

Eastern tiger swallowtail caterpillar

Lanternfly

Festive Amazon parrots

Chameleon

Shining pot beetles

Red-crowned Amazon parrot

Weevils

Lizard

Green tree frog

Bamboo pit viper

Grasshoppers

Lovebirds

Spiders

Long-horned grasshoppers

Alexandrine
parakeet

Weevils

Sunset moth

Asterope
sapphira
butterfly

Fire-tufted
barbet

Red-eyed
tree frog

Iguana

Figeater
beetles

Plumed basilisk

Amazon parrot

Red-eyed tree frog

Green
tree frog

Australian
green tree frog

Rabbitfish

Blue-green chromis

Red-eyed
tree frog

Lanternflies

Monkey
grasshopper

Iguana

43

Going green

Green is a useful color when you need to hide in the forest. How many green insects, birds, and lizards can you find hiding in these tricky puzzles?

Spot the difference

Can you find the three differences between these two caterpillars?

GREEN FUR

This sloth looks green because of algae growing on its fur. It helps the sloth to hide from predators.

Matching pair

Find the two identical beetles below.

Color me in

Use different shades of green to color in this butterfly.

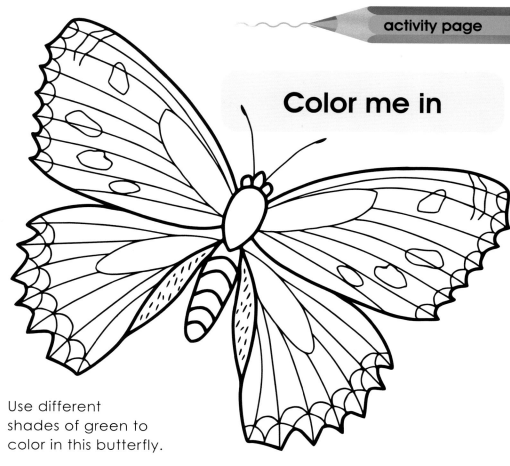

What comes next?

Look at the patterns below and work out which green creature comes next.

Use your stickers here!

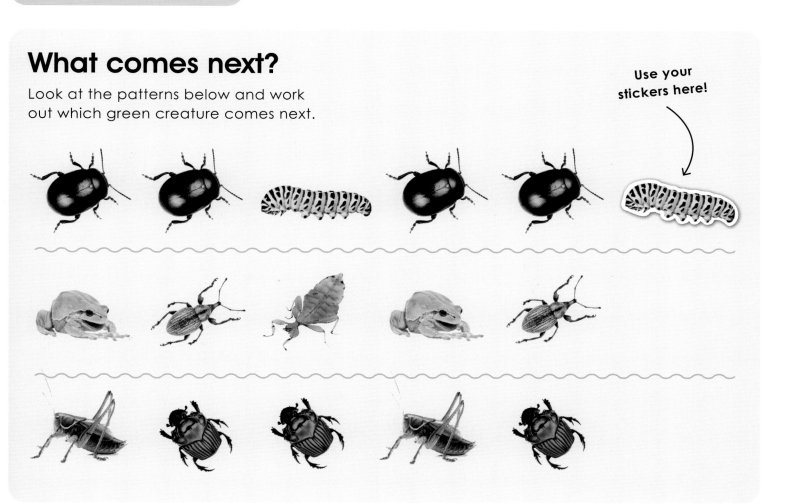

Find the cricket!

The red-eyed tree frogs all want to reach the delicious cricket.
Which one gets the tasty snack?

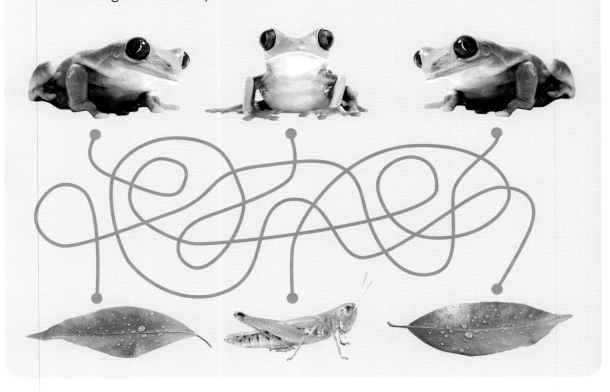

Which one has the most?

The parrots have found some crunchy nuts. Which one has the most?

WAIT AND HIDE

The green tree snake hides among the leaves. It keeps still and waits for an animal it wants to eat to pass. Then it pounces!

What's missing?

One of the luna moths is missing a spot. Can you spot which one?

Snake snack

The snake is looking for its dinner. Look at the shadow. Can you see which animal it has found?

Blue

Blue is a color used for showing off on land, but in the sea it is used for blending in. The fish in this huge shoal match the blue of the water, making them difficult to count. Their enemies, such as sharks, find it tricky to pick them out to catch and eat.

Dart frog

Blue tits

Blue crayfish

Longhorn beetle

Violet ground beetle

Macaw

Blue-crested lizard

Leaf beetles

Violet ground beetles

Woodboring beetles

Jewelry beetle

Weevil beetles

Betta fish

Blue discus fish

Blue spotted fish

Powder blue tang fish

Victoria crowned pigeon

Tropical fish

Morpho butterflies

Morpho butterfly

White-bellied redstart

Green sea turtle

Damselflies

Dragonfly

Sea slug

Sea slug

Sea stars

Peacock

Blue-spotted salamander

Leaf insects

Dung beetle

Unicornfish

Blue parrotfish

Electric eel

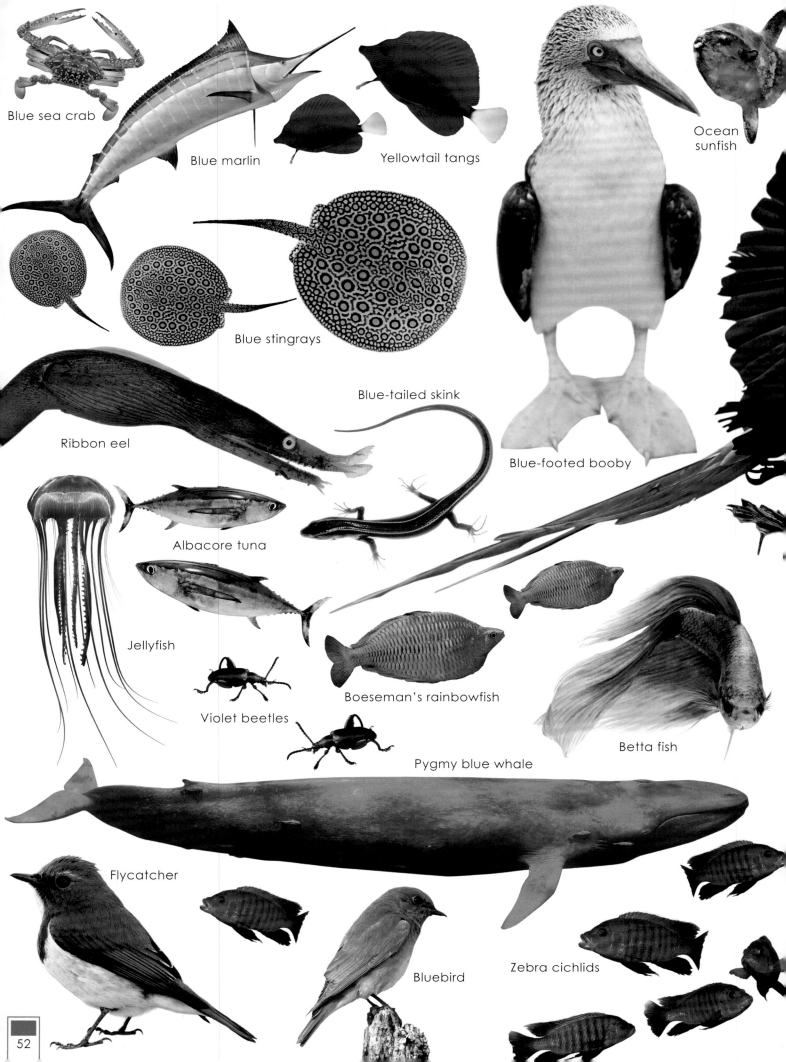

Blue sea crab

Blue marlin

Yellowtail tangs

Ocean sunfish

Blue stingrays

Blue-tailed skink

Ribbon eel

Blue-footed booby

Albacore tuna

Jellyfish

Violet beetles

Boeseman's rainbowfish

Betta fish

Pygmy blue whale

Flycatcher

Bluebird

Zebra cichlids

52

Common blue butterflies

Bluebird

Masked lovebird

Sea slug

Blue lobster

Macaw

Damselfly

Betta fish

Boxfish

Parrotfish

Betta fish

Betta fish

Black-crowned
night heron

Parrotfish

Blue jay

Bright blue

Dive in to these puzzles to find out which blue creatures live underwater, which live on land, and which fly high in the skies.

Sticker scene

Find the matching parrot fish sticker on your sheet, and add it to the coral scene. Can you find any more blue fish?

Use your stickers here!

BLUE FOOT

The male blue-footed booby dances on its blue feet to attract a mate. The brighter the blue, the more impressed a female will be!

How many left?

Each water lilly can only have one dragonfly land on it. How many dragonflies won't be able to land?

Rescue the chicks!

The blue jay is trying to get back to its nest. Can you help it?

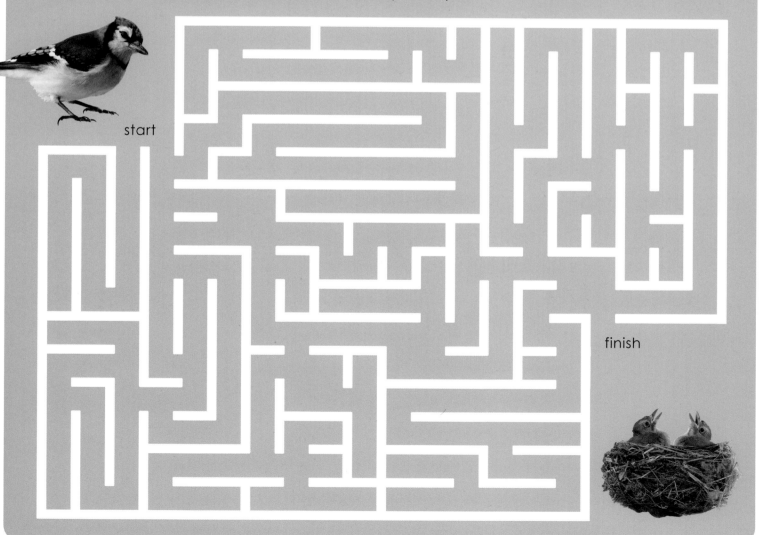

start

finish

Follow the lines

The blue shark is hungry. Which line must it take to reach the blue tang?

Jellyfish

Sea slug

Blue tang

DAZZLE AND HIDE

Blue morpho butterflies are bright blue when they fly. When they close their wings they are completely brown and camouflaged!

Odd one out

There is one beetle that is different. Can you spot it?

Draw the other half

Can you draw the other half of the flying parrot?

Match the shadows

Match the blue animals to their shadows.

Butterfly   Hummingbird   Starfish   Fish   Lizard

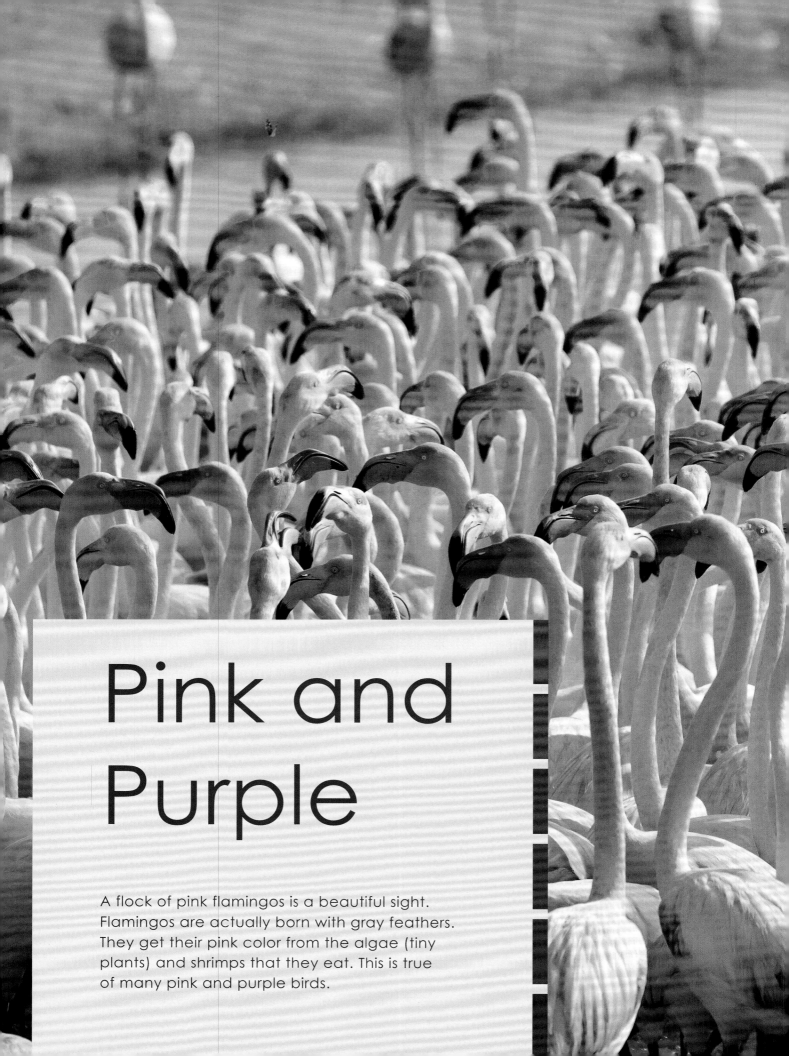

Pink and Purple

A flock of pink flamingos is a beautiful sight. Flamingos are actually born with gray feathers. They get their pink color from the algae (tiny plants) and shrimps that they eat. This is true of many pink and purple birds.

Pink butterflies

Phasmatodea

Elephant
hawk-moth

Roseate
spoonbill

Pink butterflies

Sphynx
cat

Anthias

Pygmy
seahorse

Sea
stars

Orchid
mantis

Japanese macaque

Sawfly
larva

Flamingo

Pig

Sea mollusk

Flamingo

Scallop

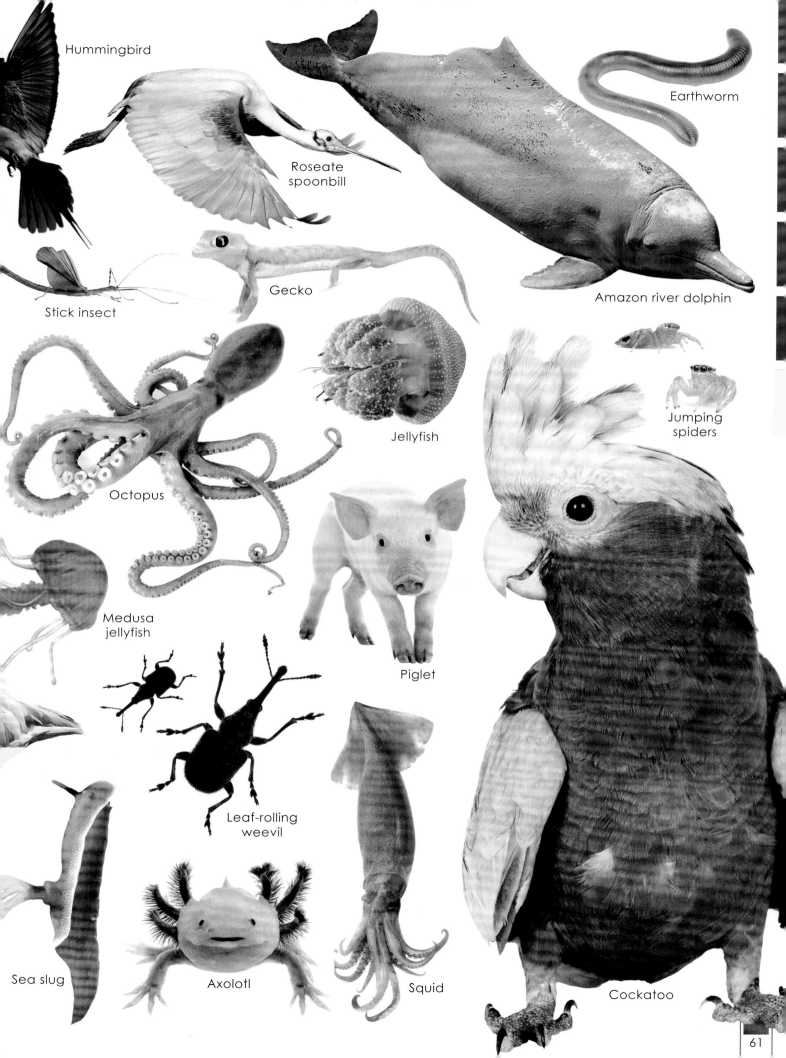

Hummingbird

Roseate
spoonbill

Earthworm

Stick insect

Gecko

Amazon river dolphin

Octopus

Jellyfish

Jumping
spiders

Medusa
jellyfish

Piglet

Leaf-rolling
weevil

Sea slug

Axolotl

Squid

Cockatoo

Pink puzzles

There are lots of flying pink creatures in these pretty pink puzzles. Find the answers before they flutter away.

Matching pair

Look at the fluttering butterflies. Can you find two that are the same?

ALL CHANGE

Baby flamingos are white when they are born. The food they eat makes their feathers pink!

Color me in

Use different shades
of pink to color in
this hummingbird.

What comes next?

Look at the order of the animals and
work out which comes next.

**Use your
stickers here!**

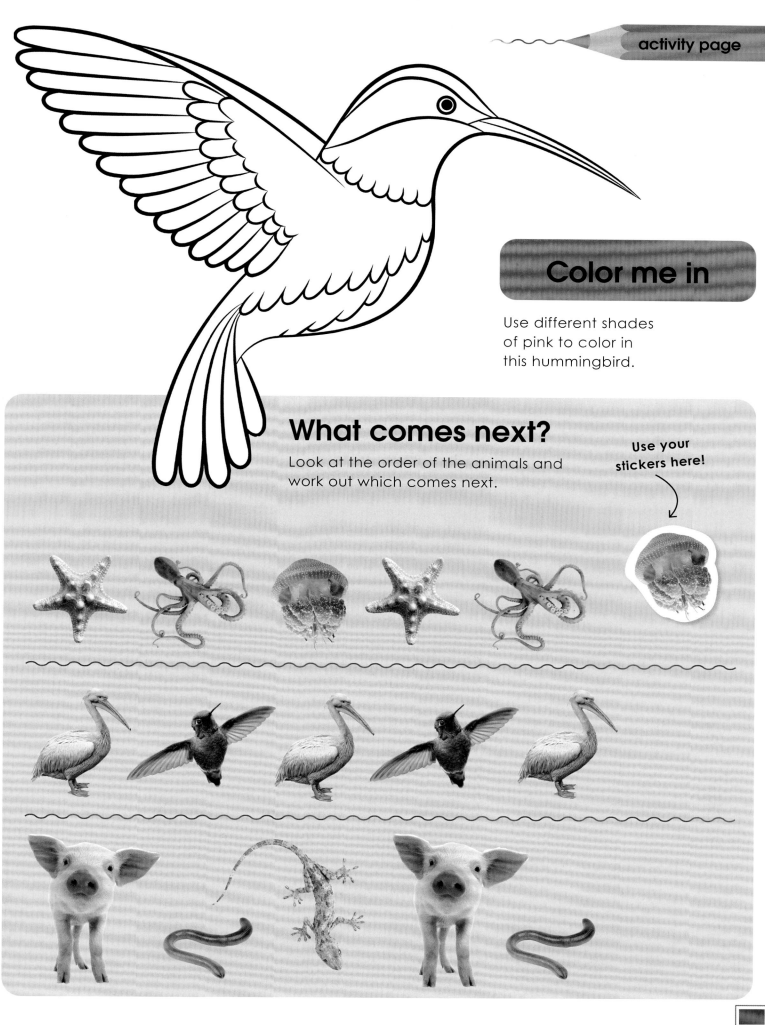

Bats

Butterfly

Sunbird

Sand dollar

Octopus

Humphead wrasse

Butterflies

Sea urchin

Scarab beetle

Darkling beetle

Tropical fish

Yellowfin surgeonfish

Giant clam

Salamander

Hoopoe

Shiny cowbird

Staghorn coral

Hoopoe

Flatworm

Betta fish

Sea stars

Poison dart frogs

Butterflies

Sea slug

Violet sea snail

Parrotfish

Hummingbird

Sea urchins

Tropical fish

Tropical fish

Scarab beetle

Brush-footed butterfly

Orchid mantis

Flatworm

Macaw

Butterflies

Blue tangs

Hummingbird

Dragonfly

Spanish shawl sea slug

Purple patch

Do you love the color purple?
What is your favorite purple
animal? Can you see it on this page?

Sticker scene

Use your stickers here!

The purple butterfly loves these purple flowers.
How many more purple butterflies can you find
on your sticker sheet to add to the scene?

ROYAL PURPLE

Bow down to the purple emperor
butterfly! It got its name because
purple is a royal color for
emperors, kings, and queens.

Word search

Can you find these purple creatures in the letter grid?

m	f	i	s	h
a	r	m	t	s
c	o	r	a	l
a	g	v	e	p
w	c	l	a	m

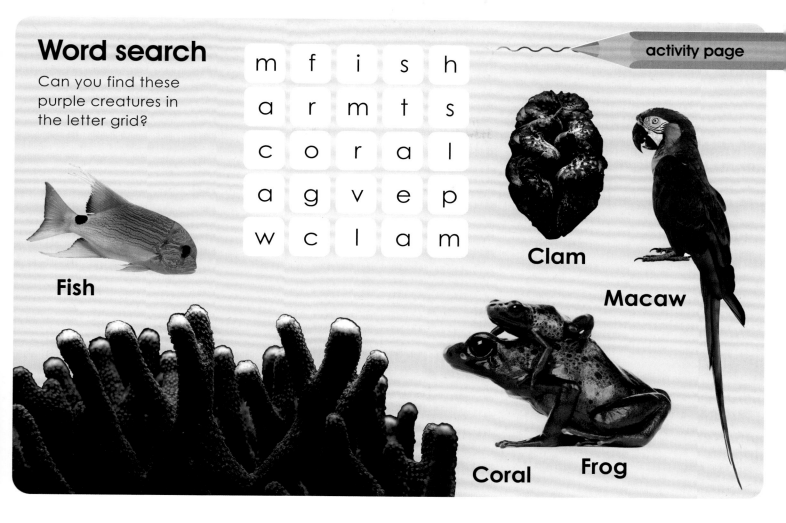

Fish

Clam

Macaw

Coral **Frog**

Ocean commotion

Only one of these creatures will find the coral. Which one is it?

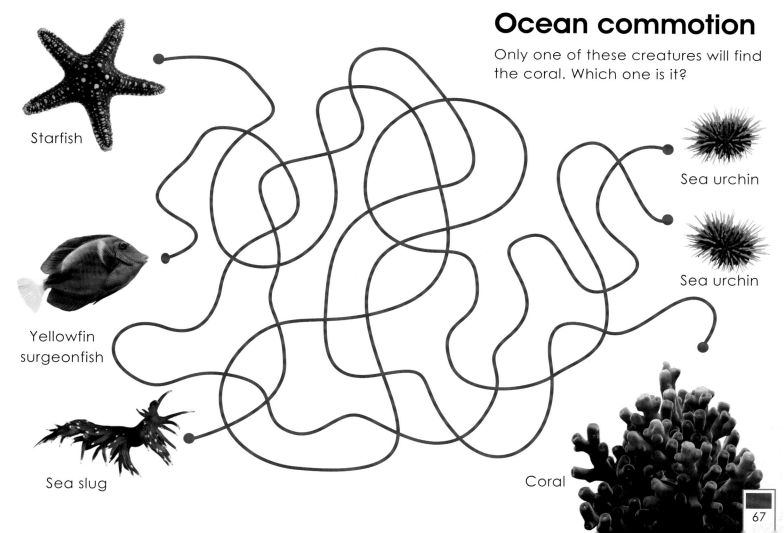

Starfish

Sea urchin

Sea urchin

Yellowfin surgeonfish

Sea slug

Coral

Brown

Animals that live in woods, deserts, or on the ground are often brown to blend in. It's tricky to spot the brown insects rushing around among these dead twigs and leaves.

Praying mantis

Silkmoth

Eagle owl

Bactrian camel

Pheasant

Wolf spider

Snail

Toad

Leafwing butterfly

Hedgehog

Katydid

Greenbottle blue tarantula

Redknee tarantula

Stick insect

Red deer

Duck

Russian tortoise

Grasshopper

Song thrush

Mantis

Owl

Caterpillar

Stag beetle

Rhinoceros beetle

Crested gecko

Red squirrel

Amazon tree boa

Diadem butterfly

Rabbit

Cricket

Pheasants

Amazonian bush cricket

Millipede

Meerkat

Turkestan cockroach

Red Kangaroo

Joey

Butterfly

Hedgehog

Giraffe

Brown bear

Box turtle

Scorpion

Grapevine beetle

Moorish gecko

Leaf insect

Longhorn beetle

Bush cricket

Mole cricket

Cricket

Arab mare
and colt

California
sea lion

Rabbit

Stink
bug

Red kangaroo

Gelbvieh bull

Llamas

Red setter

Penguin
chick

Red panda

Eagle
owl

Steppe
eagle

Grizzly
bear

Darkling
beetle

Chafer beetle

Caracals

Alpacas

Stag
beetle

White-tailed deer

Shetland pony

Fruit bat

Chow chow

Trout

Cricket

Shield bug

Orb-weaver spider

Moth

Goat

Moth caterpillar

Leaf mimic katydid

Silkmoth

Indian black antelope

Cat

Viper

Ants

Wild boar piglet

Moorish gecko

Grapevine beetle

Centipedes

Sonoran desert toad

Snail

Orangutan

Golden brown

Brown is the perfect color to hide against the ground or in trees. Can you hunt out the camouflaged animals in these puzzles?

Dot to dot

What is slowly walking across this page? Connect the dots to find out.

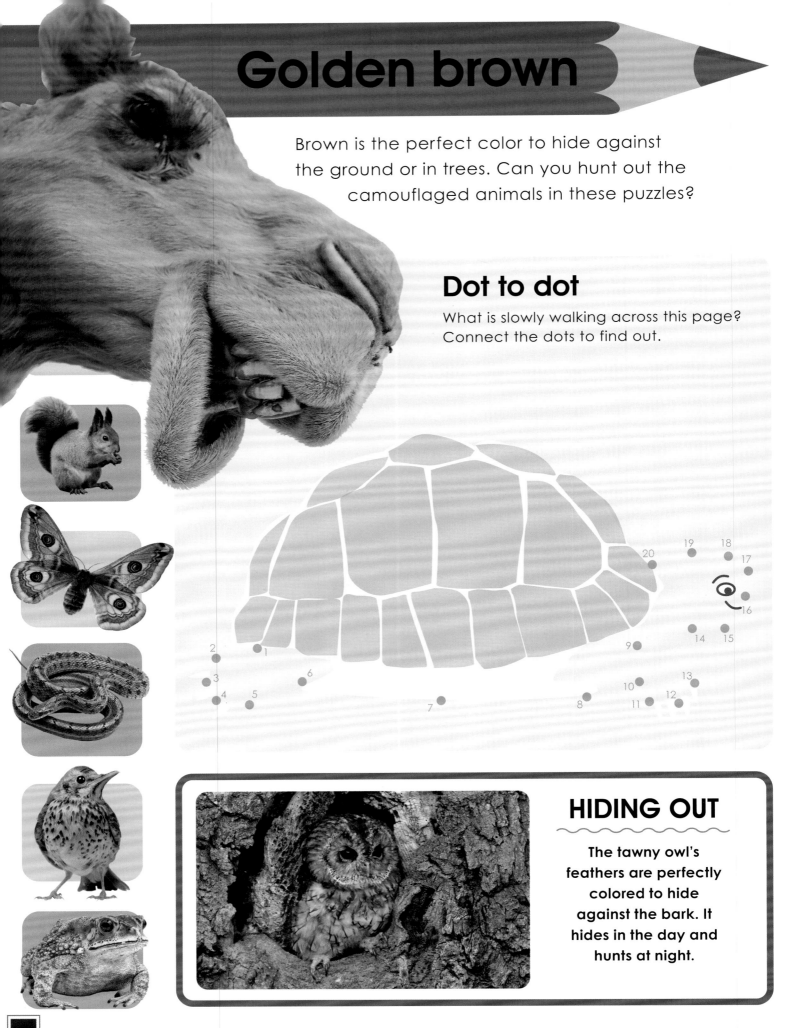

HIDING OUT

The tawny owl's feathers are perfectly colored to hide against the bark. It hides in the day and hunts at night.

Find the matching pair

Can you find two spiky hedgehogs that are exactly the same?

Shadow search

Look at the shapes carefully. Match each animal to its shadow.

Spot the difference

Can you spot three differences between these giraffes?

Black, White, and Gray

Zebras have stunning black-and-white coats. Their striking colors help to put off flies. It seems that the biting, blood-sucking flies don't like landing on the dazzling stripes. These stripes also confuse predators, by making it hard for them to see individual zebras within the herd.

Aquatic salamander

Scarab beetle

Grass snake

Horse

Scorpion

Butterfly

Tasmanian devil

Flower beetle

Angelfish

Transvaal girdled lizard

Labrador retriever

Dolphin

Oil beetle

Giant anteater

Black wildebeest

Southern ground hornbill

Fire-bellied newt

Egyptian cobra

Great
mormon
butterfly

Telescope
goldfish

Rock monitor
lizard

Mole

Indian
bison

Sea
urchin

Butterfly

Ant

Stag beetle

Skate

Red-tailed
black shark

Chimpanzee

Minotaur
beetle

Cat

Dog

Armored
beetles

Bess beetle

Angelfish

Clownfish

American bison

Curlyhair tarantula

Giant
snakehead fish

Ferret

Leopard

Alpine
newt

Peacock
moth

Leaf
beetle

Rhinoceros beetle

Butterfly

Minks

Italian
mastiff

Giant Panda

Black moor
goldfish

Humboldt
penguins

Curlyhair
tarantulas

Sea lion pup

Bonobo

Jackdaw

Black widow spider

Rook

Rook

Bald eagle

Horned beetle

Gorilla

Griffon vulture

Magpie

Rooster

Ferret

Orca whale

Sturgeon

Carpet beetle

Pot-bellied piglet

Llama

Earless seal

Stag beetle

Black

A black animal is perfectly hidden at night. How many black animals can you find in these puzzles?

Word search

Find the black creatures hiding in this word grid.

d	o	g	s	h
c	p	l	e	o
f	b	e	a	r
d	x	w	l	s
s	n	a	k	e

Snake

Horse

Bear

Dog

Seal

DARK LEOPARD

A panther is actually a leopard! Its spots are so dark that you can't see them well. It hunts at night so it is completely hidden.

What comes next?

Can you work out which animal comes next on each line?
You will find them on your sticker sheet.

activity page

Use your
stickers here!

Panda puzzle

The panda is hungry.
Help it to find the bamboo
leaves it loves to eat.

start

finish

Tamandua

Pyrenean mountain dog

Rat

Humboldt penguin

Alaskan malamute puppy

Butterfly

Albino American alligator

Cabbage butterflies

Snowy owl

Hamster

Mute swan

English bulldog

Tortoise beetle

Crowned sifaka

Maltese puppy

Emperor penguin

Albino deer

Goat and kid

Betta fish

Ermine

Bigeye fish

White lion

Fly larvae

Albino kangaroos

Hedgehog

Turkey

Butterfly

Cow

Rat

Caribou

Arctic fox

Valais
lamb

Flamingo

Stork

Snow
leopard

Gerbil

Arctic
fox

Coral

Brahman
calf

Saiga
antelope

Betta
fish

Albino ferret

Siamese kitten

Moth

Doves

Parrotfish

Capuchin monkey

Butterfly

Duck

Barn owl

Hedgehog

Albino kingsnake

Guinea pig

Pyrenean mountain dog

Butterfish

Chicken

Albino ball python

Bald eagle

Maltese puppy

Humboldt penguin

Fire goby

Jezebel butterflies

Ermine

Kid

Snow leopard gecko

Green tree frog

Kid

Cockatoo

Fly lavae

Crowned sifaka

Gibbon

Clown knifefish

Persian cat

Rabbit

Humboldt penguin

Striped skunk

Rat

Siberian husky puppy

Sheep

Giant panda cub

California kingsnake

Duck

Cabbage butterfly

White

White can be bright! But if animals live in the snow, white feathers and fur hides them perfectly. Can you solve these white, wintery puzzles?

How many left?

Only five ducks have laid their eggs. How many ducks do not have a nest?

COAT SWAP

The Arctic fox is white in the winter to hide in the snow. In the summer it changes its coat! The fur turns brown to hide it against the ground.

Find the bear twins!

Help the polar bear mom find its two cute cubs.

Matching pair

Only two of the butterflies are the same. Can you spot the matching pair?

Oil beetle

Ant

White-backed vulture

Dove

Buzzard eagle

Sphynx kitten

Rabbit

Goose

Giant anteater

Greater kudu

Koala

Owlet

Desert horned lizard

Komodo dragon

Grey crowned crane

Warthog

Short-nosed unicornfish

Pufferfish

African grey parrot

Tapir

Pufferfish

Giant anteater

Otter

Sphynx cat

Scottish fold cat

Hippopotamus

Coypu

Weimaraner

Chinchillas

Wolf

Rat

Jackdaw

Short-nosed unicornfish

Seagulls

Macaque monkey

Verreaux's eagle-owl

African pompano

Tinselfish

Cow

British shorthair cat

Foureye butterflyfish

Andalusian horse

Kiwis

Tawny frogmouth

White rhinoceros

Rhinoceros

White-faced owl

Snowy owl

Clymene dolphin

Jackdaw

Aardvark

Pig

Arctic fox

Chinchillas

Cockatiel

Hawaiian gosling

Dwarf hamsters

Herring

Hippopotamus

Pangasius

Bottlenose dolphin

Raccoon

Whale shark

Stingray

Poodle

Bonnethead shark

Cockatiels

Alligator hatchling

Giant anteater

Heron

Rat

Raccoon

African grey parrot

Ferret

Lop-eared rabbit

Wombats

Scottish fold kitten

Kangaroo

Komodo dragon

African elephant

Asian elephant

Mole

Tiger shark

Warthog

Florida pompano

Sugar glider

Silver barb

Rats

Japanese macaques

Multi-colored

Many animals are multi-colored or have striking patterns. This allows them to hide from their enemies by matching patterns of light and shadows in nature, but can also be a way of standing out from the crowd.

Parrot

Chameleon

Chameleon

Pink-necked
green pigeon

Red-eyed
tree frog

Guppy

Macaw

Parrotfish

Masked lovebirds

Red-eyed
tree frog

Banded
pitta

Mandrill

Clown
triggerfish

Budgerigar

Peacock

Sea slug

Lorikeet

Blue-crested
lizard

European
bee-eater

Gouldian finch

Parakeet

Titan triggerfish

Spanish shawl
sea slug

Sulawesi
hornbill

Dung
beetle

Butterfly

Hummingbird

Mandarin
duck

Lanternfly

Weevil

Jewelry
beetle

Tree frog

Spotted
sweetlips
fish

Woodboring
beetle

Macaw

Betta
fish

Woodboring
beetle

Blue tit

Mandarin
fish

Kingfisher

Boeseman's
rainbowfish

Queen
angelfish

Tropical fish

Butterflyfish

Betta
fish

Sun
parakeet

Hoeven's
wrasse

Poison dart frog

Comet

Egyptian
green toad

Snowy
owl

Monkey
grasshopper

Stingray

Dalmatian puppy

Eastern baton
blue butterfly

Sea
slug

Pheasar

Asian
water
monitor

Gecko

Coral
trout

Helmeted
guineafowl

Koi

Giraffe

Ladybug

Litchi bug

Hyena

Gecko

Speckled kingsnake

Cheetah

Stingray

Pygmy
seahorse

Coral
trout

Comet

Woodboring
beetle

Spotted lady beetle

Harlequin sweetlips

Jaguar

Millennium gold discus fish

Asterope sapphira butterflies

Fire salamander

Stink bug

Butterfly

Butterfly

Longhorn beetle

Scarab beetle

Telescope goldfish

Snow leopard cub

Leopard

Black-head snake

Corn snake

Ladybug

Leopard slug

Grouper fish

Locust

Ladybug

Coral hind

Deer

Clown triggerfish

Weevil

Pigeon blood discus fish

Machaon caterpillar

Jumping zebra spider

Butterflyfish

Lemur

Emperor angelfish

Lionfish

Redknee tarantula

Emperor angelfish

Clown fish

Striped shield bug

Snail

Bongo antelope

Blue-crested lizard

Centipede

Longhorn beetle

Tiger barb

Honey bee

Zebra

Cat

Jewelry beetle

Vulturine guinea

Wasps

Woodboring beetles

Sea slug

Hungarian milk snake

Snout beetle

Panther chameleon

White Bengal tiger

Jewel scarab beetle

Checkered beetle

Oriental sweetlips

Woodpecker

Striped spider

Poison dart frog

Rosy boa

Bumblebee

Caterpillar

Sugar glider

Copperband butterflyfish

Clown surgeonfish

Zebra spider

Multibarred angelfish

Tiger

101

Multi-colored

If you are still deciding on favorite animal color, this is the page for you. It's multi-colored mayhem!

Can you find them?

What a lot of flying colors! Can you find 3 parrots, 2 yellow butterflies, 2 blue butterflies, and 1 ladybug?

COLOR CHANGE

Chameleons can change the color of their skin! When they feel excited, the colors become brighter.

Sticker scene

Look for some multi-colored fish on your sticker sheet to add to the reef. How many can you find?

Use your stickers here!

Color me in

Color in the striped lizard.
Use as many colors as you like.

Odd one out?

One of the butterflies is slightly different.
Which one doesn't match the others?

Color Works

The three primary colors, red, yellow, and blue, can be mixed together to create all the colors of the rainbow. If you are lucky and you spot a rainbow in the sky, you will notice that the different colors blend into one another, creating a beautiful image in the sky.

In nature, animals most often match the colors around them to stay hidden, but if they were all to come out and show off, they would make a magnificent living rainbow.

The next few pages explore different animals and their amazing colors. There is an animal for every color you can imagine! And even more, there are animals of every shade of every color. How many different blues can you count? How many more can you imagine?

Let these animal rainbows inspire you to notice all the colors in the world around you.